T0193566

Save Me the Last Dance

Save Me the Last Dance

James R. Dixon

SAVE ME THE LAST DANCE

iUniverse books may be ordered through booksellers or by contacting:

iUniverse
1663 Liberty Drive
Bloomington, IN 47403
www.iuniverse.com
1-800-Authors (1-800-288-4677)

Because of the dynamic nature of the Internet, any web addresses or links contained in this book may have changed since publication and may no longer be valid. The views expressed in this work are solely those of the author and do not necessarily reflect the views of the publisher, and the publisher hereby disclaims any responsibility for them.

Any people depicted in stock imagery provided by Thinkstock are models, and such images are being used for illustrative purposes only.
Certain stock imagery © Thinkstock.

ISBN: 978-1-5320-3294-3 (sc)
ISBN: 978-1-5320-3293-6 (e)

Library of Congress Control Number: 2017916083

Print information available on the last page.

iUniverse rev. date: 10/25/2017

Looking For Love

For a while now I've been on a search to find
That special woman who takes control of my spine
With a soft touch and voice so genuine
Someone I can exceed eternity with and stand the test of time

My quest began in my area. No one of interest was around
The girls I've settled for made me end up on the ground
So I traveled far to a land where the wishes were consistent
Thinking a new environment would make things different

After years without success I felt like a tainted wishing well
After all the deposits I've made I still continued to fail
I say "failure is not an option". But I may have to accept it
It's like finding a job in a recession. Opportunities are limited

There's someone for everyone. It may not apply to me
Am I meant to be alone? Will I ever be free?
Of just making friends and break free of the suspense
Of me trying to find real love; will the journey ever end

After all of my shortcomings how do I remain confident
One told me "don't be so demanding and dominant"
So the adjustment I'll make is to stop pressuring me
Stop looking for love and let love find me

Noelle

5'5, brown eyes, big breasts, thick thighs, beautiful skin
Haven't spoken a word, my attraction begins
I don't know much about you. I just imagine
Your beauty has me curiosity driven

You clean up nice! I appreciate your fashion
You're extremely beautiful! Have you entered any pageants
Are you materialistic; jewelry, luxury cars, mansions
If I lived in a trailer would you still be interested

Although conversations with her were genuine
I'd rather have you in the end! You're my constant
This poem says everything I can't tell you in person
Under different circumstances I could explain my attraction

Senryu Intermission

After looking for
love in all the
wrong places, somehow
I found you

First, allow me to say "you're extremely beautiful"! Now I know what you're thinking. Here's another sleazy compliment from a man who has no chance with me. However, all of your relationships to date have ended in apathy. Imagine a night with me; Candlelit dinner overlooking the beach and stimulating conversations between you and me. Can you subscribe to the theory?

Body Like Heaven

What must I do for you to imagine a night with me?

I'm lost without you and my vision is discrete!

I can't describe the sex drive I had
Once entering the pearled gates
The same can't be said
About others you used to date
I'm intrigued by your mind state. I can relate
To every word you whisper in my ear
You have me saying words I made up
As I penetrate you burst into tears
In fear that I'll leave you
But my feelings are impossible to disappear
Sometimes they go when you blow my mind
But they quickly reappear
I try to serenade you with them
But thoughts of stroking your body would interfere
As I massage your body
While kissing you below your ear

What must I do for you to imagine a night with me?

I'm lost without you and my vision is discrete!

Say I Love You

How do I tell you **I love you**
  Without saying I love you
  Without saying I trust you
  Without saying I lust for you

How do I tell you **I'm needy**
  Without being clingy
  Without being creepy
  Without being greedy

How do I show you **I miss you**
  Without kissing you
  Without gripping you
  Without stripping you

How do I show you **I love you**
  Without touching you
  Without hugging you
  Without fucking you

Senryu Intermission

You're everything
I never knew I
wanted. You claimed
that I was too.

For weeks our conversations were in full swing. Despite her apprehension, we've talked about everything. Maybe her avoidance suggested she had ulterior motives. But what she thought I let go unnoticed was the fact that the same fight I put on display for her was reciprocated by the same men that left her hurt.

Fight For Me I

Fight for me

Like you fought for the man who would invite you to
expensive dinners only to leave you stuck with the check

Fight for me

Like you fought for the man who only viewed
you as his personal sex object

Fight for me

Like you fought for the man who would rather
have you be less than your best

Fight for me

Like you fought for the man who stripped you
of your pride, dignity, and self respect

Fight for me

Like you fought for the man who flirts with other
women in front of you with no hesitation

Fight for me

Like you fought for the man who took another woman
on what should've been your birthday vacation

Fight for me

Like you fought for the man who cheated
on you when you were pregnant

Fight for me

Like you fought for the man you bailed out of prison

Excuses

I grew up a dyslexic kid

Walked over and disrespected

A talentless fawn

Swimming in a pond of contraceptives

From day one I was teased

I was never shown love

Mistreated as if I was obsolete

Ostracized for birth effects I had no control of

Suffering from facial disfigurement

I walked with my head at a tilt

To look slightly normal since

My body was unstably built

Senryu Intermission

Although forgiveness
is laudable, it
serves as my
biggest weakness

What is it about her that makes me tolerate her excuses? Truth is, I never met a woman so ruthless. She was truth-less, but benevolent. Compassionate as she defended men who indulged in activities that were illegal. But as her and her accomplice walked passed me, she was the lesser of the two evils.

Walked Passed Me

I'm struggling living the life of a starving artist
Mailbox of unpaid bills. Two months from getting evicted
Faulty plumbing in the bathroom. No food in the kitchen
Low book sales. I thought my career was finished
But in an instant, I felt replenished
The minute she walked passed me

Out of desperation, I took a different woman on a date
She pleaded to leave. I begged her to stay
Agonizing thoughts of her with him wouldn't go away
My life was in complete and utter disarray
But to my dismay, all of that went away
The day she walked passed me

I fell for a different woman who was cunning and forthright
She changed! My disappointment in her lasted a fortnight
Investing time in her was the biggest mistake of my life
I was worried my love interest wouldn't forgive me twice
But in a blink of an eye, everything was alright
The night she walked passed me

Bouquet Of Roses

I hand delivered you
a bouquet yesterday.
Along with an assortment of
milk, dark, and caramel chocolate.
Sprinkled with a gift.

With each petal signifying reasons
why I like you,
you could pick roses all day.
It was all worth it
to see a smile on your face.

Even though it lasted
for all of two minutes.
Upon reading the card,
I saw a sheer look of disappointment.

Maybe reading "Sincerely James"
at the bottom put you in shock.
Maybe you thought I had
a part time job at a flower shop.
Maybe you thought the man and woman
standing atop the card was photo shopped.

Nevertheless

You snapped back into reality
to think again that
everything you envisioned romantically
you don't receive in him.

Senryu Intermission

Hold on! Wait!
According to you
this isn't the nature
of a man

So you thought your boyfriend, the jerk, the parolee, the prison inmate, the man who verbally degrades you, the man who physically assaults you would shower you with love and romance. Did you really think he was capable of being a gentleman? The thought of it is laughable, hilarious, preposterous, and ludicrous!

You Were There I

I sat atop a mountain
Beneath the lighthouse
Overlooking an ocean of scenic views
Lamenting; yet documenting
My devotion to you
Panicking as hurricane like winds
Causes erosion
While fleeing for higher ground
My body bounces off rocks and
Quickly cascades into the ocean
Gravitational waves pulled
My body towards the shore
When I felt life as I knew it was no more

You were there, not her!

Deformed and disfigured
Some looked at me different
Some viewed me as inept
Some viewed me as a hindrance

You were there, not her!

You Were There II

When some dissected my
Emotional diatribes
Then used them to taunt me
And hurt my pride

You were there, not her!

You were there
Every time I needed you most

You were there
When my shadows felt like ghosts

You were there
When family and friends turned their backs on me

You were there
When women took advantage of me

You were there
When my ex-girlfriends ditched

You were there
To deliver me from that psycho bitch

You were there
Through my depression and abuse

You were there
When they all lied about the truth

You were there, not her!

Senryu Intermission

Your mannerisms
and behavioral
patterns are odd,
weird, bizarre

Just when I thought I had you all figured out, I'd learn something new. You have the decency to put your selfishness aside to care for someone other than you! Could this be our long-awaited, highly anticipated breakthrough?

In Lust With A Dream

I fell in love with reality

But you were in lust with a dream

I fell in love with you

But you fell in lust with an actor

For you my heart was free

He played you! He coerced you to think

He supported everything you've dreamed

You fell in lust with your dream of a

Beautiful home, husband, children, and family

Those four things in your dream

Could've been brought to reality

Had you invested in me

When I told you "I love you"

To hear "you love me too"

Is what I thought I would've heard

But the expression on your face

Told the story of my naive heart

That couldn't be said in words

I was in love with you

But you were in lust with a dream

Take the sum of that dream; those four things

Subtract the children, remove the family

Then all you'd have left in that beautiful home is me

But that's not a life you envision

Fight For Me II

Fight for me

Like you fought for the man who's remorseless
about being a pathological liar

Fight for me

Like you fought for the man who stole your car, preventing
you from getting to work, causing you to get fired

Fight for me

Like you fought for the man who verbally assaulted
you for questioning his whereabouts

Fight for me
Like you fought for the man who packed up your
belongings and kicked you out of your own house

Fight for me

Like you fought for the man who disrespected your family,
insulted your culture, and mocked your traditions

Fight for me

Like you fought for the man who beat you down then called
the cops claiming he assaulted you out of self defense

Fight for me

Like you fought for the man who for marijuana trafficking
is now serving a twenty year prison stint

Fight for me

Like you fought for all of them

Senryu Intermission

Some say "pain is
love"! I say "at what
point does love have
to become pain"?

The love I have for you is strong enough to move mountains. I'm oblivious
as to why you don't feel the same. You complain about your man profusely!
When given solutions, you make excuses for him. You're a track star
running the same circle game.

With Him

If you're really happy with him
Why pursue me
Confide in me
Cry over me

If you're truly in love with him
Why slander him
Complain on him
Defame, shame him

If you feel he's the man for you
You would claim him
Not flirt with men
Not act stupid

False Expectations

You

Expect

Perfection

Sorry to say

I'm far from perfect

My problems extend from

Anger, rage, and temperaments

Child abuse and abandonment

Jilting the aspects that creates love

Soft touch, kisses, conversations, and hugs

Try Someone Different

You tried dating the **Manipulator**
Who would run guilt trips
To spin things in his favor

You tried dating the **Player**
Who changed women more
Than he changed his underwear
You were number 69 year to date
On the list of women
He treated unfair

You tried dating the **Athlete**
Who'd spend more time in the mirror
Than you'd spend maintaining
Your hair, nails, and feet

You tried dating the **Parolee**
Who wore more jewelry on his ankle
Than you did on your whole body

You tried dating the **Sex Addict**
Thinking you could rehabilitate him
Then reap all the benefits
Until he cheated with his
Three ex-wives and his mistress

You should try someone different
Maybe you'd get different results

You should try dating the **Teacher**
Education is his best feature
An upstanding civilian
An inspiration to children

You should try dating the **Entrepreneur**
A business man who is influential
With unlimited earning potential

You should try dating the **Personal Trainer**
A man who can healthily
Enhance your mind,
Body, spirit, faith,
Confidence, and appearance

You should try dating the **Creative Writer**
The artist, the poet
The hopeless romantic
A man who can express
His feelings towards you
Via words enchanted

You should try someone different
Maybe you'd get different results

Senryu Intermission

When I'm around you
I freeze. I lose my
train of thought. My
knees get weak!

Did I ever tell you how much your connection with him made me mad?
He cheated on his wife with you. Oddly enough, although he was married,
you were the best thing he ever had.

One Day

One second I like you
and the next, I despise you

One minute I await you
and the next, I hate you

One hour you break bread with me
and the next, you're dead to me

One day I'm in love with you
and the next, I'm done with you

When She Hugs Me

When she hugs me

I could feel her vulnerability
Her lack of motion
Her dehydrated body hunched over; broken
Her eyes welded up with tears of resentment
She's subconsciously contemplating
The years of her life she wasted with him

When she hugs me

I could feel her warmth
Her sense of comfort
Her lethargic body relaxed; reformed
Her heart is open to receiving love again
She's mentally hell bent on
Not recreating a similar situation

Missing You

Although we've never been on a date
Never had a conversation that whisked me away
Never talked personally to connect or relate
I'm standing here missing you

Although we've never shared a lustful hug
Never admired the scent of your perfume while rubbing your butt
Never experienced a magnitude of your love
I'm sitting here missing you

Although we've never shared a kiss
Never had a night of passionate, intimate bliss
Never caressed your breasts, or licked your clit
I'm lying here missing you

Senryu Intermission

When you hug me
I can feel our
connection. I know
you feel it too

Captivating, breathtaking! All synonyms of beautiful, you are! I'm falling for you hard. My feelings for you are strong. They're too explicit to recite from a hallmark card.

Fight For Me III

Fight for me

A man who will be honored and privileged to have you in his life

Fight for me

A man who would love to stand across from you
at an alter and nominate you as his wife

Fight for me

A man who could help you raise a family

Fight for me

A man who would be a prominent figure in his
children's lives and not a dead beat

Fight for me

A stable man who exudes humility and integrity

Fight for me

A man whom in life you can enjoy the finer things

Fight for me

A man who will love and cherish you without taking you for granted

Fight for me

A man who will defend, protect, and stand
by you through thick and thin

Best Friend

The thought of having you as my best friend
Started out as a fantasy

Which instantly became reality
Once I was blessed to feel the warmth of your hand

When introduced to you
I felt feelings I didn't understand

The power of the anointed one
Ran through my body

Making me the chosen one
To play a tune in his band

After backsliding multiple times
I had to start all over again

With God directing my future
The resurrection of my past began

Familiar places brought back familiar faces
Meditation provided inspiration to fix old relationships

Now I'm back and saved again
Feeling better than I ever did

But no other feeling felt better than the one I felt
After nominating you as my best friend

Senryu Intermission

I can give you
twenty-five reasons
why I'm really in love
with you!

Women think I'm an easy target. Some think I'm weak and vulnerable. Some think I'm susceptible to taking in anything, including their bullshit. When we first met, I was damaged. I was brainwashed by previous mistakes. I was a novice. But you should've taken a chance on me anyway.

25 Reasons

I can give you 25 reasons why I'm really in love with you:

One
The mystery behind your brown eyes

Two
Your voluptuous body and thick thighs

Three
The scent of your perfume that colognes the air when you leave a room

Four
Your affectionate greetings

Five
The anticipation of your affectious smile that tugs on my heart strings

Six
Your eclectic wardrobe that accentuates your curves

Seven
Your patented death stare you give when I get slick
at the mouth and loose with my words

I can give you 25 reasons why I'm really in love with you:

Eight, Nine, Ten
Your consistency, nurturing personality, and motherly spirit

Eleven
Your high self-esteem and opulence

Twelve
Your support of my depression when others didn't want to hear it

Thirteen
Your lack of tolerance for other people's bullshit

I can give you 25 reasons why I'm really in love with you:

Fourteen
Five years later you still get me erect

Fifteen
You have the same effect on me that you did when we first met

Sixteen – Twenty-five
Is for all the men you could've pursued, but you considered me instead

Our Dance

Save me the last dance

Our dance
Can be atop a mountain in the middle of the winter in 30 degree temperatures

Our dance
Can be in 100 degree weather in the Sahara desert

Our dance
Can be the night after you cut ties with your ex-boyfriend

Our dance
Can create unification your friends and family can't comprehend

Save me the last dance

Our dance
Can be in the middle of the rain

Our dance
Can be strong enough to survive a tornado and a hurricane

Our dance
Can be passionate and lead to us swapping saliva

Our dance
Can be minutes after I ejaculate in your vagina

Save me the last dance

Our dance
Can be at our wedding

Our dance
Can be on the balcony of our honeymoon suite

Our dance
Can be after the birth of our offspring

Our dance
Regardless of geography can and will be elite

Previous Release

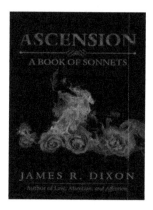

How much of yourself can you give to another person before you feel empty? Through all the blood, sweat, and passion, love can sometimes feel hollow especially when the enthusiasm is not reciprocated. Written in Japanese Senryu format, Ascension is a novella in verse that tells the heart-breaking story of one man's unfortunate tussle with unfair love.

Previous Release

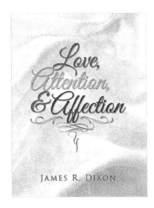

Love, Attention, and Affection is a three part story elaborating on my trials and tribulations in relationships. It is comprised of three individual stories. But, collectively the three stories combine to tell one ultimate story. Each individual story is represented by a particular color that generalizes the emotions and sentiments of the story. Love is represented by red. Attention correlates to yellow. Affection is strongly associated with purple.

With this book I aspire to ignite healthy conversations with people as to what essential functions and components are necessary in order to obtain and maintain a successful relationship.

Previous Release

Broken Silence presents a collection of very personal poems that get to the heart of who author James R. Dixon is and what he has to say. He believes that sometimes the quiet ones have the most to say, but getting others to hear them can be a problem. Being different can mean that you may find yourself explaining your actions to others.

Broken Silence is also his breakthrough collection explaining his thoughts and feelings on relationships and other personal issues. These poems seek to offer hope and inspiration to others who are struggling to find themselves.

Previous Release

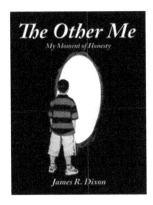

The Other Me presents a collection of very personal poems by author James R. Dixon. It is based on misconceptions placed on an individual's personality. He feels as though many people have been perceived a certain way by others and for the most part, those preconceived notions are wrong. With that said, that puts people in the position to have to defend themselves against those who misjudge them. "The Other Me" is his self-defense.

Printed in the United States
By Bookmasters